DE-ICED

Susan Wicks was born and grew up in Kent and studied French Literature at the Universities of Hull and Sussex. Her *Night Toad: New & Selected Poems* (Bloodaxe Books, 2003) included a new collection with selections from three earlier books published by Faber: *Singing Underwater*, winner of the Aldeburgh Poetry Festival Prize; *Open Diagnosis*, which was one of the Poetry Society's New Generation Poets titles; and *The Clever Daughter*, a Poetry Book Society Choice which was shortlisted for both T.S. Eliot and Forward Prizes. Her latest collection is *De-iced* (Bloodaxe Books, 2007).

She has also published two novels and a short memoir, *Driving My Father*. She has lived in France, Ireland and the U.S. and held writing residencies in North America and Europe. She is Director of the Centre for Creative Writing at the University of Kent, and lives in Tunbridge Wells.

SUSAN WICKS

De-iced

BLOODAXE BOOKS

ISBN: 978 1 85224 755 3

First published 2007 by
Bloodaxe Books Ltd,
Highgreen,
Tarset,
Northumberland NE48 1RP.

www.bloodaxebooks.com
For further information about Bloodaxe titles
please visit our website or write to
the above address for a catalogue.

Bloodaxe Books Ltd acknowledges
the financial assistance of
Arts Council England, North East.

Cover design: Neil Astley & Pamela Robertson-Pearce.

Cover printing: J. Thomson Colour Printers Ltd, Glasgow.

Printed in Great Britain by
Bell & Bain Limited, Glasgow, Scotland.

ACKNOWLEDGEMENTS

Acknowledgements are due to the editors of the following publications in which some of these poems have already appeared, sometimes under different titles: *Acumen, Critical Quarterly, Cyphers* (Ireland), *Magma, Mslexia, PN Review, Poetry Calendar 2006* (ed. Shafiq Naz), *Poetry Ireland Review, Poetry London, The Rialto, Smith's Knoll, The SHOp* (Ireland), *The Times Literary Supplement* and *La Traductière* (France).

'The Meat Thieves' won a Commendation in the National Poetry Competition, 2003.

'Beside the Tracks' was written as a commission for the 27th Festival franco-anglais de poésie in Paris in June 2004 on the subject of 'La Trace et l'oubli'.

I am extremely grateful both to the MacDowell Colony and to the Virginia Center for the Creative Arts, where a number of these poems were written, and to the other writers and artists I met at MacDowell, whose work I found so exhilarating.

Special thanks too to my first readers, Caroline Price, Mara Bergman and Moniza Alvi.

CONTENTS

The Meat Thieves

Drivers wanted. Thieves and alcoholics need not apply.
JOB AD IN A BUTCHER'S WINDOW

And yet we're good with meat.
Our agile fingers know how to pick
a crusted lock. Corn-fed chickens wait
quartered in the cold safe
in a fur of breath. Under our coats
we hide small finds – an ear, a stiffened wing,
a wishbone; rabbits' kidneys slide their satin eyes
into our pockets where the fluff congeals.
We can tiptoe through blood
and leave no footprints: friends will testify
we were far from this square of sawdust,
far from ourselves.

When we first saw meat
swing from your hook our hands started to shake
as we reached for the bottle. Now we stroke apart
the cutlets on their spine of bone. The marbled fat
is cool, the suet clean as candles;
mince curls like hair
from the greased machine. And each discarded heart
is a maze of hidden chambers, every valve
gasps open. In a gold wave
the sawdust swells underfoot:
all we can take is ours

and the getaway car waiting,
packed tight from roof to floor
with perishable goods. We'll part the air
in a screech of burnt rubber. While you turn in your sheet
we'll stitch up your town
with a zigzag of tail-lights,
hooting and whooping at a job well done.

9

La Manière de jouer au Diable

Fr: **diable** – *Eng:* **devil; diabolo**
(from a display at the Het Labyrint estaminet, Kemmel)

Just at the outer corner of the Devil's eye
a man is fishing. He angles his twin rods
and the line goes taut – something rolls and slides
jumping, opens its round mouth
in an O of terror, while in the centre frame –
no doubt about it here – a man is fishing
men. Notice the movement of his hands,
his flexed wrists, the stance
and you'll find yourself grinning
through a mess of tangled hair.
The horns will start to sprout
at your temples, two of them upturned
and two that curl like rams' – and then a tail
to swish at flies with, tufted like a cow's.
And once you've learned to change
direction at the crest of your two-handed wave
here's something to practise on
in earnest – a whole glass-fronted display
of precious objects: brown ceramic; green
and crackle-glazed; blue as sky
and full of holes like a candle-holder; wood
or copper, pewter. Bone
with blood and muscle. Set him on your wire
and move your arms in sequence
till he rolls from side to side
like a sea-sick dumb-bell. Toss him in the air.

Larks

(July 2005)

If the sky falls we shall catch larks.

PROVERB

For two days we have been finding larks
in strange places. They flutter and hop
maimed into doorways, scatter feathers,
blacken the city's trees
with their smoke-breath song.
Even underground

the earth is full of them. No one goes in or out
without stepping on wing-bones,
squashing a puff of air
from their morello lungs.

They litter our houses, slide in stinking piles
too heavy to sweep up.
Their beaks open and shut
between our fingers. Their eggshells fill our laps.

For two whole days
a lark's been sitting on my chest
and trilling silence,
skinning the whole black sky
with its bald sound.

Beside the Tracks

They must be everywhere, lying asleep
in holes or ditches, or crumpled like foetuses between
the rotting sheds that crouch close to the line.
In darkness they wake
to scale a concrete cliff or squirm through a chain-link fence
to do their night writing. Their intricate names
balloon into spaces, lean in like lovers
till the wall of a red-brick cutting, a bridge's whole span
is a hash of flattened snake
in blue or silver. From the last train
you might just glimpse them, someone's shaking back
turned to your window as his right arm
works up and down
while the ball-bearing rattles in its can.

Sometimes you almost hear it – the spurt and hiss
of colour on rain-streaked concrete
under the platform's grey lip
or a disused signal-box – the same blind word
endlessly repeated: an inflatable Technicolor god
with his eyes squeezed shut. What could be a B
stares out between rolls of fat; an L digs its sharp knee
into a hoarding's corner; an S is a bloated arm
wrenched from its socket. Yet there's no name
you could say aloud, only a curl of paint
like a flattened cushion, a coiled spring.

Then one day you read a line
in the local press – how one of them fell
to a bed of cinders and broke his neck
or slipped on a live rail
and sent out a spark
that lit up a whole street. Or a passing train
wiped him from the wall like a wet leaf
from a windscreen, before his last word was done.

And you're the trespasser here. You're the wrong race,
the wrong gender. No wonder you can't understand
the language, the stylised dance

of characters high on a wall
where no one but birds can reach.
When you raise your hand
there's no one to hold the torch;
your own scribble of paint
still floats in the night breezes, waiting to land
on a piss-stink underpass or railwayman's hut.

Only in sleep
does the mist come down
sweetly as raindrops, and mean
more than a starred expletive from a lost cartoon.

Crane

It swings towards you, lacy as a wing,
its criss-cross of steel string stretching
as if from your own childhood.
Or is it some kind of clock
made out of sunlight, that perfect equivalence
of weight and counterweight as the heavy load
lowers itself behind the backs of houses?
You try to put a name to the ache:
it's not beauty exactly, not the tight throat of grief –
but it seems to move
for no reason, so that watching it you move too,
a part of you swinging out
into nothing, while the you on the ground
looks up and sees itself
and shivers, nailed to the blue sky.

This is how God would be
if he were a migrant worker in this town
and whimsical, taking any shape he chose –
a white suspension bridge, a beam
of splintered light, the neck of a skeleton swan
not parting the lips of clouds
but laying itself down
as if on water – putting in time
slowly constructing something we can't see
between rooftops, something that rises stone by stone
from an infill, a plot of brown-field land.

How trite is that? If you go up close you'll see
there's a wrecker's ball swinging. Okay,
so let God be a crane –
it's as good a disguise as any, apt as a bull or swan
or barn-born baby –
but you ride him into nothing
and the walls come down.

Man on a Traffic Island

Flat early morning light.
A hundred yards ahead
where town meets open country
a man steps out
and stands and waits.

There's something wrong –
he's hunched, one arm held stiff,
the elbow bent –
he's less than himself
or more. His crippled shape
comes nearer, bigger,
almost on me, when the hump

opens its wings – a bird,
the pinions high as the man's head
and flexing – filling my whole sky
with feathers. As I drive
I'm thinking, falcon, goshawk, eagle,
vulture, not finding the right name.

Where can they be going
hungry for the rush
of small escaping things
in the early morning?
The path that rises here
in suburbs leads to flat fields

and ends at the river
where the way's overgrown
with nettles and a man
whistles for his bird's return.

The Sky Horses

We're caught under glass. The road's hot breath
surrounds us, truck-wheels come close enough to touch.
Sunlight on steel, a transporter hammers by
while at my nearside wing the poplars shrink away
shivering in a Mexican wave and I drive
through a swirl of leaves. Ahead, this glitter-stream
of metal bodies. On the news
a man's voice swells half-heard in a phrase
from Tel Aviv or London as the traffic shimmers, roars
towards the next junction, bunches and slows.

And then, ahead of us but still too far away
at first to make out, a bridge looms closer,
and inching in single file from left to right,
three horses in silhouette
and the riders, hatted, erect
and graceful, are picking their slow path across the sky.

A moment and they're gone, we're underneath
and through in a stink of diesel – but they still walk
delicately onwards, treading the narrow span
from south to north. The horses lift each hoof
and replace it, the unseen reins lie slack
over the smooth necks: behind and above us the young
riders, hair swinging, nudge the warm flanks
and move on, clicking their soft tongues.

On the Road South

Northern Lights

Imagine a pale green liquid
rippling on the glass of your window,
a blush in the bottom corner
that used to be flame or sunset.
Imagine the light running
on the pane in a sudden fountain,
the glass cold under your fingers,
the sky unbroken, icy.

Imagine the greens of snow,
the blues of a trapped river,
a street's defiant welcome
passing in a flash of neon.
Outside, a town's breath freezes,
the curved rim of the mountains
glitters to the horizon.

Beyond this snow-swept place
the people walk in greyness.
You unroll your bed, stretch out
with your hands behind your head
to watch this Arctic night
wheel on its brightest stars,
and the show only beginning.

Sausalito

I imagine you free-wheeling
down past a string of harbours
to a view that falls suddenly open,
where you step down to the floating sidewalk,
tread gently on the oiled ripples
down a street of tethered houseboats
rocking in a maze of water.

In these small wooden rooms
fridges hum behind lace curtains,
a cat licks its paw. Upstairs
a china dancer spreads her white thighs.
A man sleeps with a long-empty
Bud can crushed between his fingers
while on the screen another
cracks eggs. Outside, a child drops pennies
between the slats; she crouches
to watch them shimmer, lose themselves
in dark. A floating garden
holds a woman half-naked
in a blaze of impatiens, tied
to the mother boat. As you walk by
her shadow sways,
the child looks up,
follows your spreading circles with her eyes.

I imagine you cycling back
across the Golden Gate as if on a tightrope,
wheels cleaving to the windy cordage,
pedalling first forwards then backwards,
a parasol open above you
like a rose. I see you climbing
the hill of the strung cable
where you'll bow, the crowd beneath you
swaying, faces slick with sweat;
I see you lifted
high on a wave of cheering
as you step off on to the tiny platform.

Copper Canyon

Either it runs like this:
rails snake along the valley floor
as creepers reach out to snare
the smoke from your rackety train;
voices bounce backwards and forwards
till the rose of the canyon falls open
on sky; from far above
through steam the tongues of light
glisten in the sun's pink slit –

or like this: you're in full sun,
your shadow rippling across the rock-face,
a bird's high nest, a clinging tangle
of roots – while four thousand feet under
there's an unseen cleft
crowded with leaning trunks
where cold- and warm-blooded creatures
fuse to the branches as the sun sinks.

Darling, it's getting late.
The gorge flushes blood-red
as birds rise screaming, gather
up there at the head of the canyon
where the two lines meet.

Spa Valley Railway, New Year's Day

The steam surrounds us, inevitable as fog,
catching in the bare branches.
Like one of those afternoons
when the platform would all but disappear –
a flat world you could fall off the edge of,
lights coming at you faintly out of nothing.

They used to send us home
so we could get back before night fell
and we'd vanish into mist, leaving only our voices
amplified by damp, the stamp
of unseen feet, the sudden clank of a signal.

Now as we walk back
we are any family
on a New Year's outing, our feet heavy with earth:
the husband strides ahead,
the daughter's too-long jeans trail in the mud,
the mother struggles to keep up
as mothers do.
   Oh, what am I now
but heart and lungs and boots,
a small circle of hood,
rain on my skin, hunger? The train
comes chuffing past across the hillside,
puffing out smoke
and steam to mist the windows and roll under,
writing its steady signature.

In a Wing-mirror

True, you can see yourself
if you lean over slightly – a face
that ages as you age, a section of fringe
that's longer or shorter, changing from brown to grey
and dyed back, skin at the corner of your eye
more wrinkled than you thought. And also your life
streaming away behind you with the hedges,
dusty, illegible as the signs.

But in the back
two kids are strapped into child-seats –
two little girls
asleep, or paper white,
about to be sick. Or playing with some toy
you've forgotten the name of, sucking their thumbs
or middle fingers, or singing a song
or just dreamy, watching the shapes of trees
and trucks flick past, as they twiddle a muslin square
against their noses. And then they're gone –
and you're alone with grey upholstered seat-backs,
reflecting that this is what mirrors are for –
to watch the future in
without turning round, while you stay out of view.

But sometimes in the glass, remember
how they'd meet our eyes
and say, 'How far is it?' and we'd pretend to know.

Sky, Cloth Cap, Little White Car

At Seven-mile Lane I catch a glimpse of them
ahead of me in a small white car
that's not quite a Micra: she has permed grey hair
and a pale mac; he's in a cloth cap, and they're not
my dead parents, or not quite.

Then they turn off and I'm driving alone
under a fading sky
that's not quite molten metal, that stops its gold spokes
over the flying fields for a moment,
and my throat aches

for them, who are not quite the last
of the old couples in the little white cars.
Their cloth cap, their steel-grey curls
are penultimate things, already accelerating away –
his veined hand on the gearstick,
her box of tissues on the dash
just in case – you never know
what's round the corner – while the sky
washes my windscreen orange with its last light.

After Rain

I round the bend to find
the oncoming traffic
stopped unaccountably behind
a small green van. What
has arrested it
here in this gleam of sun
on tarmac? Is he stuck?
He doesn't frown,
he isn't trying to restart
his engine. Can he have broken down?

He waits at the wheel, serene
while inches in front
a duck
waddles across. I catch his grin,
reflect it back
as I drive on
to a blare of baffled horns
through a lake of sun.

Man on the Seaton Tram

How old was he – in his sixties?
It was hard to be sure, with those ill-fitting
teeth he scrunched his face tight on,
his eyes that were like a child's,
seeming to look up in wonder
and follow passing branches.
And the T-shirt with CALIFORNIA
stencilled in white, chosen
on his behalf. He never even smiled.
Perhaps his shut face
didn't rise to smiling. He was like a child
just doing as he was told. And the day
blazed past us, trees and wooded hills,
the estuary's spread fan
of open water, where we could see fish
just under the surface, swimming upstream,
herons like old grey men
hunched on the islands, a buzzard
fixed like a finial to a post.
And air blew through the open tram,
ruffling the hair on our bare arms
as we clattered on, rocking
towards the Colyton terminus,
the last loop of the line.

When they stood up I saw he was a little guy –
no bigger than my father. I saw how they touched his back
as he left the tram. How this was what was left
and his empty eyes
still following light along a branch –
this and the big fish swerving, swimming against the tide,
the breathing clumps of weed,
the statue-bird that passed us, motionless,
the bird lifting and grazing water as it flew.

Dream
(to Bridget)

You only had to leave and your bedroom
has rolled out into space
in a swirl of branches where the full moon
presses its pale face to the glass.
There's a pool of milk under the sill.
I'm paddling in white blood
that dries without a trace. A trail
leads from the curtain to the made bed

where something of you still lies
looking up at these posters – a man on his knees
slick as a seal in his blue latex sheath;
a ripple of ochre desert; a gold-silk-trousered Puck
pinned in mid-leap with a message: Back
in forty minutes; the spinning earth.

Mobile

Above me a house is moving downhill
on a lorry, headlights on in the rainy afternoon.
I can hear it from here, the low moan
of brakes as it moves forward
like someone blowing across the open end
of a length of metal tube, the empty rooms
all slipping imperceptibly down
past the line of picture windows,
rocking slightly, shuddering as the wind
catches them broadside. All that stainless steel
and hardboard, those cupboard doors
sliding from side to side along their dusty grooves,
the bench-seats' pads of foam,
all easing quietly away
to that single note. Think of them inching by –
the fold-down table for the fish and chips
where children watched TV and heard the sky
explode into rain, drew faces in breath
misting the windows, till they grew up and left.
Think of the fraying curtains and the wire
that stopped them swaying stretched
between two hooks, the blackened pan
they fried their bacon in –
those cubes of air
edging away on a lorry, no one now to own
that smell of rust and seaweed
I remember, Calor gas and damp and perished rubber,
Calomine on pads of cotton-wool to stop the burn.

Lady with the Unicorn

Musée du Moyen Age, Paris

For years they've kept her here
in darkness with her bowl of sweets,
her portable organ, her careful crown of flowers

under this artificial moon
to live out her sentence in an embroidered field
of lilies, tasting the intricate fruit

while through her looking-glass
he admires himself, the slowly emerging shape
of a perfect stallion at grass.

Now he stands and waits.
She strokes his horn, and his ears go goatish,
his muzzle elongates.

Is there no end? The stoat, the fox, the heron,
the monkey with wicked eyes
remember another time

before they were brought here torn
and threadbare, when a tide of rot
rose through the stitches of the horn

like water round a marker, till under the flag
with its flowing crescents only her hand
flowered on the pale tip,

around her the bowl and circlet bobbing,
the animals one by one,
the organ chiming as the waves came in.

Picasso Museum, Paris, August

A high right nipple slides
up into shoulder
as his woman twists herself away
and won't come back. The baby's high grey eye

looks anywhere but front. The goat
dangles its belly from those thongs of skin.
Inside, a weight of stones
or emptiness. A woman lies
like a vase, toppled on her side.

What is it? What
has left its negative
painted in almost-black –
its own image cut out?

Even the guitars
are getting thinner, a few strings
stretched from what we understand
as keys to sounding-board. *Thrummmm!*

The horse-girl startles,
whinnies at me, flares
the deep, dark crawl-space of her nose.

The man in the bronze armchair

is fucking it senseless.
Holding on for his life
he tenses his polished buttocks
and the chair rises to meet him,
raises her chiselled thighs,
en pointe like a dancer
resting on stunted arms.

What an attractive line
they make, these two together,
their smooth arc
of juncture sheltering his ribs
or hers. Their double face
is a single open mouth
like a hippo's, gaping on a yawn

or something straining to walk –
a tortoise, thrusting its wizened neck
in folds of flesh from the collar
to see how the world looks.

And yes, how slow they are
to reach a climax. How slow love is.
In days or years
they'll still be here
unmoving, buttocks and back and crown
in the same pure curve,
grizzled with pigeon-droppings
while the mower
buzzes around them over the parched grass.

Jacques Lipchitz, Le Cri, *Tuileries*

Coolies, Mishima Pass

Hokusai, 'Mishima Pass in Kai Province' (print)

The mountain breathes out smoke
in a long-drawn, sleepy sentence:
blue floods the high slopes,
bleeding into tree-trunk and crevice
while far below
a lather of bubbles floats
foaming like soap or blossom –
someone's rising thought.

What are you incubating, ink-blue god of trees
and mountains, steadily seeping down?
Your trunk's unshaven, your boulders are eggs of fleece.
What do these pelts and parallels mean?

But wait
and look again. The suds are human –
so many people moving about their business
under their hats.

One Can Sing It
Jo Smail: etching, 14 x 14.5 inches

in nine pink-painted triangles;
black-wing nose-bird, pecking

in air, in little skin, in pennants;
the last clinging of black blossom

in mountain-snow and air and is it sunrise;
in giant crowfoot, black meeting

in petals drop by drop
and rose, and white endlessly surrounding

in white of rising breath, pink to the horizon;
the one black note sustained beyond breathing

in slur of ink and pawprint out of nothing:
pink in the making.

Paper from Korea

On a surface like this you could paint anything
with a soft brush, following the fibres
that float already in the translucent paper
like veins in leaves or insect wings through water.

You could go with it or against it,
in pools of liquid gold or knives of shadow,
painting what is already visible
and stirs in each breath from the window

until you've found the knot, the shape that lives
behind the grain. Now what you paint
is what you're painting on. You touch your brush
to paper, and the tree moves.

Charolais

In the night rain the cows are creamy
ghosts of themselves, separated by a dark curtain
from what they were in daylight, as if they'd lain down as calves
and woken thirty years later
to dark. With the torch we pick them out.
A cow turns its head and its eyes shine
milky, unblinking. And they come ambling uphill
as if we brought good news – coming to listen
to your soft Wisconsin voice that calls to them, tells them
it's safe to sleep, tells them how we listen each evening
to their mooing in the long green shadows.
How could they not understand?

It's nearly thirty years
since we first met, in this foreign country,
tasting each others' accents
with the wine. Now we inch our way back in darkness
down the blind lane where glowworms
light caverns in the wet hedges
and the cows stand watching, and the smell of the earth rises.

Laundry

So we're walking, the four of us, sweating,
early afternoon between close hedges
and sun rippling on the melting tarmac –
washed up in this other landscape
where behind a fence in deep shadow
a cock flaps his wings and eyes us
from a straggle of dusty chickens,
shaking his comb. And somehow
we find ourselves laughing, talking
hen-parties, women with other women
for a wild weekend in Blackpool
with vodka and male strippers
on the eve of somebody's wedding –
till Ken chimes in about Homer
and a gaggle of Phaeacian maidens
on some beach washing out their undies,
Odysseus in the white lace water
gasping for breath; how before a wedding
they'd dunk and drub, twisting the wet linen
into ropes as thick as wrists
till the tears ran off them
and they'd spread them on sand to stiffen.

And before we know it we're all quizzing
this ancient blind-walled building
that obviously used to mean something
to the men or women of the village
and you're saying, Guess what it is.
In front, between young nettles,
a billboard of flyblown posters:
it's a room for tasting wine
under a stone roof, a meeting-place, a barn,
some shed where old men tinker
with their engines at the end of a lane –
till we squeeze through the net of brambles
to the other side and the sinks lie open.

Moss greens the empty runnel
where water used to gurgle,
the walls echoing and sweating
to the beatings and laughter and clear voices
where they pounded the wet chemises.

The Ox-house

*(Legend has it that at Berzé-le-Châtel a man and an ox
were imprisoned together to see which would outlive the other.)*

Perhaps the ox lived longer,
half-closing its sleepy eyes
as the man pounded the oak door in disbelief
and screamed, breaking his nails,
tracking the drops of moisture down the walls.
Perhaps the ox could taste green
on its heavy lips, as it trampled the man
to grape-must, the knuckles of his hands
to white powder. Perhaps it smelled the sap rising.

Or maybe the man took off his shirt
and used it as a blindfold
so the ox stumbled and half fell
from pothole to pothole, blundering against stones
in a rain of rotten mortar
till it knocked itself lame.
Here, where a man now crouches alone,
the ox opened its great mouth
and bellowed its long dying into the roof.

Or perhaps one morning the barred door
creaked open on a new space
teeming with dust-motes, both man and beast
escaped together through the earth floor,
a lock of his filthy hair
twisted to a makeshift halter, and something limping away
six-legged through the long grass.

Visiting the Romanesque Churches

The first to slip away is La Vineuse,
folded behind us in rucked green
as we drive off into the sunlight
and the old clock striking noon.

Then Massy, lying locked
in its narrow valley – Massy, where you said, Look,
put your left foot here and you can see in –
through cobwebs to praying chairs. When we were young
we'd drive like this from village to village
stopping to taste the wine.

Now we crack St Vincent open
like a pale-yolked egg.
Besornay's given up its ghost
for a handful of ordinary rooms
with empty windows. By Besanceuil it's too late

to see much more. We circle the lichened roof
admiring its pitch
till we stumble on a camper-van, two women at their picnic
wiping their mouths in the porch.

And then that pale façade split
from brow to chin. At night St Hippolyte
lies open to the stars. Only from behind
could it still be intact, the little chapel round
and perfect, fenced off, on someone's private land.

And finally Malay with its white walls
like the walls of childhood churches.
I look for a leper's squint
but there's nothing – only a gallery I climb
like a queasy minstrel, and call your name.

They've slipped like beads
through our fingers. The arches blur
to a single round arch
of nave and window – one Romanesque church
to end all churches. The way home
could take us through them backwards
to the beginning, if we had time.

Absence de Marquage

This is how it will happen –
direction Charolles, *absence de marquage* –
to the hum of a small engine:
I'm dozing, dreaming of Mallarmé,
his shipwrecks and blank pages,
while you're mulling over past journeys –
how the four of us once travelled
from Strasbourg to East Sussex
in an orange Dyane. Somewhere
we're setting out, it's morning,
somewhere our four children
haven't even been conceived yet,
somehow the future happens
in a rising shimmer on tarmac
and dust. Now we're driving faster,
air-rush at the open windows,
the blank road disappearing
between fields of cut hay
laid out in lines to dry.
And none of us sees it coming –
just a flash of sun on the horizon
and the four of us childless for ever
and twenty-eight – our windscreen,
shocked white on impact, cracks
like ice across a lake; the car ticks.

People-watching

Seals, Inner Hope

What are they doing here, their heads strung out
like urchins over the harbour wall? Their flattened snouts

are white as a pup's, crusted with crystals of salt,
as if someone had told them to keep still

and not play games. They don't even rise and fall
with the swell. Most surprising of all

not one of them manages to disappear
and surface ten yards down. They gorge themselves on air

until they die. Those moments when you break and breathe
before you dive again – that's their whole lives.

Look at them pointing. They don't even rise to bite
each other's mouths. And the starless night

that glitters greenish-brown
with churned-up sand must be unknown

to them – something they half-invent or half-remember
from when they were young, glimpsing a solitary diver

in a wet-suit, the sea-bed blurred as through a window
while we swam over, casting our sleek shadow.

Freeing the Crabs

Time to go home. On the steps at high tide
a man's releasing crabs. Late afternoon
and the wind comes riding upstream

in little waves. The mere's a field shiny with rain
and the girls are pink as piglets, podgy
with glittery motifs

under their anoraks. They peer and poke
in the slopping bucket. He shakes it upside-down
at the water, scrapes out something dark

and spidery, quick, small-bodied –
that skitters alive
before you can even see it, and fumbles to climb

and slips again and fumbles. He nudges it back
with the toe of his boot. Gulls hover,
eyeing us – the crabs and the plump kids,

ready to snatch one of us up
and make off downstream
to a beach with waves breaking, where clumps of weed

lift and spread themselves in a fan to breathe.
How long before the tide
goes out, exposes the low line

of the causeway with its bloom of barnacles, glitter
of waves breaking half across the river?
Already the count's over,

they're throwing the shreds of bait
back where they came from. We slide sideways into our seats
and start the drive uphill.

Just under water
the crabs cluster, clambering over one another.

Yar Tor in High Wind

When we arrived at the top we could hardly
breathe, the wind sucked out of us, the air
pulled out of our mouths and noses, so we saw the river
through tears, the fall of the autumn hillside
and fields and the turning trees wavered
as if under water. We had to sit down
among stones, we didn't trust our bodies
not to fall, weren't sure we knew how to balance –
the place was so high and the high wind
swept over us, whipped hair into our faces,
scoured us, passed through us, till everything
was torn from us and lifted, skimming
across miles of heather and bent bracken.

And as we came down we leaned on the wind
and found it would bear our weight.
We stretched out our limbs on air
letting our lives stream out behind us
like albumen or snot until we were blown clean
as egg-shells and laughing, and empty.

Man in a Blue Rain-cape

Here where windows dribble stains, the gutters
choked and sweating black-green,
he's in his element.
You watch him hop and flap
downhill, spreading his arms,
to wheel like a pigeon over plastic chairs
and tables; nylon feathers flutter in the wind

as he loops the loop and circles, looking for a spire
or ridge-tile where he can tuck his head
under his rainproof wing and dream
his blue migration dreams.
What can he possibly have said

in passing? What a very English bird
to fly in rain unfazed
and roost in hollow trees and wake
you in the morning with his inveterate singing.

Copper Beech

Sometimes it's something as simple as a tree,
a copper beech in April and sun
falling through branches. You catch the shiver of new leaves –
rust, russet, autumn, winter –
and your mind's wrong-footed suddenly,
white early morning
frost crackling in the sharp grass.

Sometimes you see there's no time,
no hotter, colder – that the spark of a leaf
is itself, and short-circuits reason –
how rust is the truth
of things even in their beginning
and spring comes every year to fill the new shoots up
with copper, russet, rust, and everything's dying.

De-iced

Planes hang in the air like stars
as they come in to land. Here on the ground
snow ripples across tarmac, lifts in a neighbour's jet-stream, settles
as the flight attendant brings us nuts, iced water, pretzels,
nuts again. I've read my magazine
to the final page. And the captain's messages
mean nothing: we already know the score –
it's night, we'll never manage to take off
and everything's closing. One by one
our senses desert us: the engine's our only sound, salt
the last taste on our tongues. Our bodies ache
from this one position we've no power to change.

Then we're beckoned forward by a man with two lit wands
and machines rear over us, stretching their metal necks
as if to bite or kiss – a cuboid head
with four lit eyes. It squirts us with a cloud
of white that turns our glass opaque,
then a flood of livid green, coating our wings,
our back, our body, with icy sludge. Now we're luminous green
and ugly, already powering away –
they'll never catch us.
                                    We fly up blind
for what seems years, till the cloud lets go of us and the sky
beyond our wing-tip's shot with red,
perceptibly lighter. Invisible behind us on the ground
a man in a yellow tabard works a lever
and the creature's head swings forward,
vomits a jet of spray at another plane
as the wiper grates back and forth. We're flying clean.
Our wings are silver now, flaps sliding and retracting
in a twinkle of snowdust to the sky's command.

MacDOWELL WINTER

1

Twice a week I do my day-return
pilgrimage to Canterbury, 50 miles each way –
A26, M20, A249,
M2, in rain or dark, or almost blind
with horizontal sun – up the interminable climb
of Detling Hill where every day
the little dancer dies in a pirouette, and cloud
hangs low as fog – past Maidstone, Sittingbourne
and Whitstable – until I finally arrive
high over the Cathedral with its cache of bones
preserved for centuries, that may belong
to Archbishop Thomas à Beckett or someone
else, whose name didn't survive.

2

From home to here's a good 3,000 miles
even as the crow flies. And crows
don't fly it much. What I flew into Newark on
this afternoon was a Boeing Triple Seven –
me, my Toshiba laptop, the sum of what I know
and what I probably never will know now. I'd forgotten
my necklace, my scarf – I'd have no public face, no style,
no distinguishing marks in Heaven.

But at Gatwick I found this: *coquilles Saint-Jacques*,
nine pilgrim shells as small as a baby's nails,
incongruous as faith
and as foreign, with elongated sequins like threaded fangs
and all for £1.80. When I unpack
I'll dig out my little scissors, cut away the teeth.

3

They don't seem to be getting anywhere,
driving forwards and backwards over the same few feet
of frozen ground. At this rate
it will take them years
even to reach the road where occasional cars
disappear with a hiss. They bring the blade up close
and scour the barren triangle
in front of my diamond panes of glass.
From my typing chair
I can see them even better,
barely making progress, taking infinite care
not to look in my direction. But later

I go out to find the snow scraped almost clear
and squeaking under my boots, the sky on fire.

4

(for Hajoe and Franzy)

An acre of land in Utah was what set them off
in search of something, their toy car seen from above
as if by satellite, raising a cloud of dust.
They marked their purchase out
with compass and string and water-bottles –
their rectangle of flat scrub

next to the railway with its visitation of trains
three times a day. They could have put a rock
in the driver's path – crossed sticks, themselves –
but no. They chose instead
to offer him Coca-Cola, signalled with childish waves
for a week, the man with the shaved head, the long-leg girl
in shorts, till he stopped of his own accord,
confessed his bafflement, believed.

5

(for Bobby)

They're the same stuff, the snow and Miró
projected on the high-arched ceiling
like the birth of Christ – an elongated breast
and displaced vagina; mermaid; *oiseau divin*
dancing with uplifted wings.

But the projector's eye
goes dark: we need to be blind
to hear and feel this music in its minor key.

And then Miró is back – a blizzard of black spots
in assorted sizes, translated alive
from paper to ceiling, as the sound dies

and fire runs its ecstatic tongues
along the logs in the hearth and flakes spin down
in the outside light like moths
who've lost their seeking instinct, decided to survive.

6

The only footprints are the trees'.
No birds, no deer. Tonight
no starlight even, but the dark wood's
pale with reflections. Let me sleep out here
in a house-sized snowdrift
like the pioneers.

The furnace fan clanks on
with a shudder, and I'm up
and fucking cold. I pull on my dressing-gown
and tighten the hood, I spread my coat
on the bed, and still
I'm fucking freezing. And by dawn
they've come to dig me out.
I'm lying here. The fucking plough grates up and down.

7

(for Bill)

At first you can't recognise their cries,
can't fathom what it is that keeps them alive
through the winter, can't understand the tracks
printed on snow, don't get their jokes.

Then you begin to twig – which sole is whose
and in fresh snow or frozen, whether the spoor's
still steaming. Now when the trees creak
you know the reason. There's no need to leave

and you're not leaving. Fishing with several lines,
nudging canoes up inlets, staking pelts to dry
as the speared fish sizzle into the flame
and smoke fills every pore. So you've become

Grey Owl. You cut a hole to see what whiskered face
pops up between the floorboards, what
body slimed with oil and weed hauls itself out.

8

Easy to listen to Vivaldi as I walk among
these rows of reaching pines.
His glorias light my footsteps. And Bach –
Lux aeterna, while the sun
through a fur of branches sinks gracefully down.
Take away this, and we would be
a creak of aching joints, scarf of wet breath,
birdsong.

Cum sancto spiritu. They turned the radio on
to sing you out. They didn't say
you wouldn't last the night
but I think I guessed. I wasn't brave enough
to stay and say goodbye, my hollow love,
your own amateurish tunes
long silent, already ten years gone.

9

I have migrated here against the flow,
against my instinct to stay put or fly south
to lemon groves – 'staked
two hundred miles of black night
on the chance of finding a hole in the lake'

like a bird flying by night
and day to cross the Gulf of Mexico
in a flock, too high to recognise
'even with a scope',
using its little butterball of fat
until it's gone and it starts consuming muscle.
Touch and go always.

But the shore's closer now; the few remaining trees
reach up to meet us as the light dies.

10

And now the ploughed paths
are disappearing, already through the dark
it's hard to see my way
in the fresh snowfall, but under the first tree

there's a line of hoof-marks, each delicately alone,
or a double print that mimics a heel and toe,
sometimes more widely spaced
as she cantered – the same span as my own.

At the fork I hesitate
confused. She makes the same mistake
written in snow in a sudden wide
chicane. The deer and I are running side by side

though she has gone. She veers off left
between the trees, making a soft furrow
as her belly grazes snow, where I can't follow.

11

(for Rona)

Burns Night, and Mary pipes us in, the sound
filling the great hall, vibrating in the wood
of gallery and panels. For a moment she stands
pink-cheeked, her fingers moving, while the bladder
wheezes in and out. She may be a girl
but she plays like a kilted hero. Behind her we walk,
self-conscious in our fleeces, into another world
called Scotland. When she finishes we applaud
with hoots and whistles. People are taking pictures
of how it was. Someone's pouring the wine
and everyone's smiling, humming the same tune
from Scotland. Then Scott comes from the kitchen,
loaded with dishes – pasta, zucchini, an enormous bowl
of salad dressed with balsamic vinegar and oil.

12

When I first heard a critic use the word
'occasion', I had to look it up
quickly, afraid of looking absurd.

So this was how it worked:
things that happened gave you a core of ice
that snow could cling to
making a perfect sphere
you could throw at someone.
                              But the more I go on
the poorer my life is, and richer. At the heart
is precious nothing.
                    Camus got it right –
Sisyphus with his rolled rock
and, spinning across the sky,
that blazing football that could make you pull the trigger

and why not? We die each day.

13

How when I was little and it snowed
he'd pretend to be angry – he'd say
'Curse the weather!' – turning aside
to look at me slyly. Now I can see
him standing at my window looking out
at the white path, the white garden
tapering to a point, the white-iced slats
of the fence, the snow-bank leading
to the railway, while at his elbow I
collapse with laughter.
     If we could still exist
it would be in that whirling sky
where he raises his fist
to the glass, letting the curses fly
like snowflakes, and I squeal with joy.

14

Have I ever played on a grand before? Certainly
not one like this, with free-flaking veneer
and a whole grand-shaped landscape of despair
and hope in faded upholstery.

Could it have been his? It's old enough
though the lower C
sticks and the F's a whole cacoph-
ony of warring tones. It's time the low B
was pensioned off.

But to my fingertips
it's a foreign country. Have you ever in your dreams spoken
of things that are perfectly innocuous and woken
to find your lips

throb? Even my sonatinas
ring clear and high on something intravenous.

15

Five lines you send me from your busy life –
a parents' evening; your Year 10s; light snow,
no other news. At first it seems a denial of love,
all the cockerels of Kent standing on tiptoe
on a farmyard fence, emitting a raucous croak
from their stiff beaks. *Nothing to report.*

Those thousands of fibre-optic truths
that come to me at work, how they criss-cross
in the ether high over the Cathedral roof
like bats. *Nothing to report. No other news.*
My inbox flickers with their frequencies.

No other news. I understand
what nothing means. How the squeak of inaudible voices
shrills in your ears, how you say what you can.

16

Reading Rachel Cusk

At first I couldn't get on with her at all –
something about us both –
her quaint, almost archaic style
or my befuddled wits. Then little by little I began
to find her sun-dried Sussex woman terrifying, real
and brilliantly observed, and Martin – his great cave of mouth,
his shrunken legs – the star of the whole tale.

Now her landscape of lanes and roses radiates heat
to my room in Eaves, where the furnace belches hot air
under a thatch of snow. Inside Stella's skin
there's a vein of ice that beats
with hot impulsive blood that has its share
of icy platelets. Together
Rachel Cusk and I are a Russian doll.

17

You have this vision of an ideal fire
filling the chimney with its cracking cloth of flame
like one of those machines in a fireplace-shop display
where coloured ribbons ripple upwards above a fan –

or a mature fire, one that's almost dead
even – glowing, searing the skin
of your face as you bend to poke its heart, and liquid
red courses along its limbs.

But what it turns out to be in fact is smoke
roiling through shafts of sunlight, an alarm
with sensurround screaming.
Men with spades and ladders have to come in a truck
to dig snow from your damper.
                              And now here you are
with your feet on the hearth-stone, dreaming
of open windows, that rush of air.

18

This morning my north window's a fog of white
strung with transparent necklaces,
chains where the charms hang upwards,
skin flawless and gleaming against the light.

To the West, small clots like eyes
in a clear hole at centre pane. High up,
a scattering of blossom, a child's design
for a white six-pointed star, some pale disease.

The South's another place –
a landscape of desert cacti furred
with white flowers. Snow falls as confetti.
Spiders hang webs of ice.

The porch must face east. Only the faintest white
cross-hatchings on the door, where I come in, go out.

19

i.m. Dorothy Nimmo

Before I came, I was this I-shaped space
somewhere in New Hampshire. Light from the sun and stars
passed through my body; the sub-zero air; a deer.
Under my footprints the ground froze.

This morning, nothing of me here. As if I'd already left
or died – that absence that was her, the time she joked
'I've lost my buttocks' and all I could manage to write back
was something tasteless. Well, what did she expect?

Somewhere she still hurts. As if I have become
a 70-year-old woman in her boots and beanie hat, oiled parka,
puffing out clouds of breath. But her body's gone.

In my studio someone's packing up,
writing her last few words about a frozen lake,
a chainsaw, a New York City skyline where the lights prick on.

20

Somewhere a poem hovers – perhaps in New York
against a purple sunset as the lights in tower-blocks
flick on and people returning from work
buy hotdogs and flowers
from stands, and evening papers
from a thing you put money into – a kind of clamp –
and the news comes loose in your fingers –
or in a lit interior where two people are quarrelling or making love
or a solitary woman lingers
over a glass of wine, and suddenly looks up
to see a shape that wasn't there before – something long and slim
like a flying pen. A snatch of sound –
a buzz – a voice that fades as she strains to catch
its foreign cadences, its cargo of beyond.

21

Seven of us – ice-grippers on our soles,
four plastic toboggans. Lysley tries it out
before we even get there.
                    Then Sophocles
head-first on the orange saucer.
Ivy, new to snow, travels
                almost as far as the road.

Then Devin, Michelle,
me, Julia – all sliding sedately down, grating across grit
or wiping out
              in a snowbank

                      while the low sun
steadily turns the whole sky
to orange glass.

But the white rush
that day I did it with my cousin
after they took my tonsils out
                 when that old woman died
in the bed next to mine –

You don't feel that again.

22

For me a blank field is what survives –
stubble where the discarded husks
crunch underfoot; a gang of high-school kids
in shorts and T-shirts; that underground cave
where she says she died
yet lived to tell the tale. Hard to believe
in angels, but it seems some good fairy
was at her all-American cradle, and kept her safe.

Now I tread on her lovely bones
as I sweep my cabin. Tissue, ash,
grit from the snowplough – I scoop them all up
into my dustpan. If she's looking down
she'll see me on my knees
in a scrawl of carbon. Did she light a fire
in March, I wonder? Or wasn't it required?

23

(for John; and Iris)

A bunch of freesias the colour of rusty blood
like little hearts, or kidneys – some small part
of a rabbit or cat or squirrel, quick and bursting open,
the hot life pumping up
in sprays of flowers, the new green buds
plump on the stem like peas. Next morning I'd take my leave
and you'd be too lazy even to throw them out.
In three weeks' time their skeletons will greet me,
shrivelled to almost nothing, remote.

She works with road-kills, packets of blood and fur
she empties and cleans and reassembles
over new skeletons of wire
that can jerk their paws and tails in greeting
as if risen again
to a new electric life. Their eyes flash off and on.

24

Before I came here I decided
not to write about woods and deer, snow, moonlight

in favour of something more English. But the place
itself has decided otherwise.

Yesterday as I retraced
my own white tracks, I came across

this solitary rectangle, a perfect dent
at each of its corners – what could it possibly have meant?

And then I realised: it was where I put my laptop down
when I stopped to change hands –

as heavy here
as in Tunbridge Wells or London, Paris, New York, anywhere.

25

(for Valérie)

The horseman on your card is tall and lean
and hungry: under his stone coat
you can see his ribs; his bearded chin
juts to his breast-bone. Only his broken foot

and the horse's tell us he'll never reach
his journey's end. At first I thought he was Christ
and the horse a donkey – pictured a storm of leaves
and hosannas, which the sculptor didn't suggest.

But now I see he's a pilgrim, anonymous
in an arch of fluted shells, dreaming awake
on his way to Santiago. Under his hooves

a child-sized beggar raises his right fist
as if in anger. But the way has taken
even his instincts, all his human loves.

26

Others have been here before me and I tread
in their deep footprints: a cold boot of snow
with a sole of ice. Ahead,

his low white roof, that classic herringbone
of logs at the four corners. So this was the space
he wrote his music in – less than half my own

and twice as simple. But there's a pile of wood
at the fireside, as if for a great blaze
where his piano stood.

Three tables, three upright chairs
and some kind of ancient machine
like a typewriter, though it's hard to be sure –

what with the reflection of my own face
and the frost – a forest of young firs
in Flanders lace, a flight of butterflies.

27

You're half asleep. You turn your Schlage key and the lock's
stuck fast. However you pull and push, the key's in place,
the door won't even close, and all your worldly goods,
such as they are, are there for the taking.

Someone could steal your threadbare socks,
your dirty underwear, the tops you bought in haste
from QS (£4 each – the buttonholes all yours), your hooded
fleece, the Elastoplast for when your thumbs start flaking.

Leave it. By evening someone's cleaned and oiled
the lock. The key no longer resists.
Your door opens and closes! See what happens

here as if by magic – while you sat cross-legged and toiled
in your dream of fine brocade and satin
muttering, *No more twist?*

28

Sometimes you wake in darkness and then sleep
won't come again. Sometimes your body yearns
in an itch of stars. The skin across your nape,
your knees, has turned to sandpaper, and burns

to the touch. Your eyelids scratch. Your bottom sheet's
been ploughed and gritted to a thousand icy miles
of road that end in darkness, an old crate
long-buried, blood frozen between the wheels.

But between your feet a crack of light shines –
someone's down there beneath you, also alive
and working half-naked, his muscles glazed with sweat

and through an iron grating in the floor
the heat still rises. The furnace's intermittent roar
tells you that air still circulates. You're not dead yet.

29

The icicles at my window lengthen like teeth
from the roof's melting gums, the longest two feet,
the shortest half an inch. They call to my mouth
to wrap itself round them. Taste, they say. Eat

and feel the minutes melt inside your hand –
the way in childhood I imagined seaside rock
would taste before I tried it, those weeks of sea and sand
preserved in hardness, something I could bring back.

And it was only sugar – a shocking pink stain
on my lips to make strangers turn in the street
and stare wide-eyed, as if I were a sign,
the same red name bleeding through every cut.

These are something else. As the sun rises they
are branch and needle, bark, refracted sky.

30

(for Valérie, after Edward Hopper and Russell Hoban)

From Saint-Ouen this bare New England road
has flown through the air to land
here in my pigeon-hole. The petrol-pumps glow

larger than life, while the balding man
in shirtsleeves fumbles the nozzle, turns his back
on tarmac. Where the road runs on

trees husband their shadows. But before the black
this garage throws its invitation of light
towards the verge: that near window's awake

and blazing. High on the hanging sign
an orange horse leaps, spreading its wings.
Perfect – the dovecote with its wine-

dark shingles is just like the one on Eaves,
though the colour's reversed. Last night as I walked
you were with me. Now as the sun leaves

it's almost ten in England and the chalk
cliffs undulate unseen towards a lighthouse
where you meet me in my dreams, and we talk.

31

Something has changed – a new intensity of blue,
snow melting into the air unseen,
the birch tree's shadow
turning like a sundial towards noon

and on into darkness as the horned fears step silently in
between the trunks. Over the melting grass,
through birches shedding white skin,
they close on me, tighten their blue noose
as I stand guilty in that ring of eyes.
But these

are asking nothing: a deer picks her delicate way
under my window; a woodpecker
wakes me with a sudden clatter,
flaps casually through sunlight to a new tree.

Notes

(Numbers refer to the numbered sections of the sequence.)

1. 'The little dancer' is a reference to the silhouette of a ballerina mounted on a footbridge over the A249 at Detling. The bridge was built as the result of a campaign by Caroline Hobbs after the death of her daughter, Jade, and her mother in a traffic accident in 2001.

4. Hajoe Moderegger and Franziska Lamprecht (also known as the E-Team), German video artists living in New York. The poem refers to a short video project entitled *1.1 Acre Flat Screen*.

5. Bobby Previte, New York composer. The poem refers to his presentation of his '23 Constellations of Joan Miró' released in February 2002 by Tzodik Records.

7. Bill Burns, Canadian visual artist and Director of the Museum of Safety Gear for Small Animals, 'the largest producer of safety gear for small animals in the world'.
   The legendary Grey Owl was born Archibald Belaney in 1888 in Hastings, Sussex and emigrated in 1906 to Canada, where he lived as forest ranger, guide and author of many books. He built his cabin in Saskatchewan so that beavers could enter it through the floor via 'an underwater entrance in the adjacent lake'. (www.virtualsk.com/current_issue/grey_owl.html)

9. Kenneth B. Able, *Gatherings of Angels: Migrating Birds and Their Ecology* (Ithaca and London, Cornell U.P., 1999)

11. Rona Edington, Scottish writer living in Edinburgh. The piper was Mary Cramb, kitchen assistant. The chef was Scott Tyle.

12. The references are to Camus's *Mythe de Sisyphe* and *L'Étranger*.

14. Edward MacDowell, composer (1860-1908). The MacDowell Colony was created by Marion MacDowell and her husband on their farm in rural New Hampshire in 1907 and thrives a hundred years later to inspire and support more than 250 artists in many different disciplines every year. Its roll of honour includes James Baldwin, Willa Cather, Alice Walker, Aaron Copland and Leonard Bernstein, among many, many others.

15. The University of Kent is on a hill above the town.

16. The reference is to Rachel Cusk's second novel, *The Country Life* (Picador, 1998), for which I have a sincere admiration. Stella and Martin are (arguably) the two central characters.

19. Dorothy Nimmo, poet and fiction writer (1933-2001), author of *The Wigbox: New and Selected Poems* (Smith/Doorstop, 2000) and *James Naylor* (Sessions, 1993).

21. Lysley Tenorio, fiction writer; Sophocles Papavasilopoulos, composer; Ivy Alvarez, poet; Devin S. Moss, film-maker; Michelle Jaffé, sculptor; Julia Haslett, documentary film-maker.

22. The reference is to Alice Sebold and her novel, *The Lovely Bones* (Picador, 2004), which I understand was begun at the MacDowell Colony. She was one of the many writers to have preceded me in Baetz studio.

23. Iris Adler, sculptor.

25. Valérie Rouzeau, French poet and translator of Sylvia Plath and William Carlos Williams, author of *Pas Revoir* (Paris, le dé bleu, 2002) and *Récipients d'air* (Paris, le temps qu'il fait, 2005). The visual reference is to a sculpture on the outside of the Église Saint-Hilaire at Melle (Deux-Sèvres).

26. The log cabin in question was Edward MacDowell's own, the first 'studio' to be built at what was to become the MacDowell Colony. See 14.

27. The reference is to Beatrix Potter's *The Tailor of Gloucester* (Frederick Warne, 2002; originally published 1903).

30. Valérie Rouzeau, see note to poem 25, above.
The visual reference is to Edward Hopper's *Gas* (1940) and the literary one is to Russell Hoban's novel, *Amaryllis, Night and Day* (Bloomsbury, 2002), which refers to the same painting.

31. The reference is to Flaubert, 'La Légende de Saint Julien l'Hospitalier' in *Trois Contes*.

THE GRAHAM MICKLEWORTH RETROSPECTIVE

The fictional painter Graham Mickleworth (1912-2000) is more likely to be remembered for the controversy surrounding his relationships than for the quality of his painting or the coherence of his aesthetic vision. A retrospective in St Ives in 2003 was the occasion of a commission, which I regarded as an opportunity to explore his life and values, as much as his paintings.

Nude with Peacock Feathers

She's lying spreadeagled on an unmade bed,
one leg bent at the knee. The trailing quilt
pools on the floorboards. In the blue bowl
the grapes shine softly through their skins.

Where her face should be the feathers float
their green-gold fronds, open their span of breath
over her breasts, tangle her hair
on the pillow. It's impossible to make out
how much is woman, and how much dead bird.
And there's that small scar
on her inside thigh, as if his loaded brush
has signed her with unintended white
as he fumbled and it clattered to the floor.

Should he ease her legs gently apart
and paint what he sees? When they try to kiss
his mouth fills with soft stuff,
he's breathing feathers, knotting himself up
in a storm of sneezes. If he rests his head
on her breast he can hear the high scream
of peacocks. When he backs away
she follows him with her fan of eyes.

Children Hiding

It's a study in empty space,
a triangle of sunlight on summer grass.
This is the corner of the artist's house,
lovingly rendered. Note the texture of the low roof,
the red spiders, the roses, the carefully indented leaf.
He worked on and off for years
on these interlocking bars
of trellis, each thorn and nail.
No wonder what we have is so real.
You could reach out and rap your fist
on the down-pipe pocked and dimpled with rust,
the water-butt oozing green tears.

And then you start to see them – a pair of eyes
up in the branches, a flash of yellow skirt,
a small grey foot
in a battered sandal sticking out
from behind the tub, a freckled wrist
with a watch on a sun-white strap. And before you can say Stop!
they're crawling all over you, Daddy, Daddy,
there's a child in your lap
with paint in her hair and fingers, paint on a blade
of grass, they've knocked you flying in the blue shade.

Learning to Dance

What dominates the picture is their two hands
raised in the foreground: he's trying to push her away
while her fingers curl sweetly over the cool span
at the base of his thumb. He straightens his back
under the dark cloth. From the way he holds his head
you can tell he's puzzled as she tries to lead,
speaking through her body in a braille of silk.
Here, like this. He tenses. Quick, quick. And the slow
hypnotic melody that smokes its wind-up dark
through a riff of tenor sax. Her dress flows from her thigh
as she moves, the polished leather of her pale shoe
against his polished shoe nudges him into line
till he gets it right. And then he's got it – he's leaning in
to where the light-confetti dances on her cheek,
her hair, her breasts, to where their bodies meet
and bleed together – mirrored like birches in a lake
of polished wood – and somehow he's keeping time
with her heart, his footprints fill up with flame.

Hot Sand with Cherries

Even without the title, you can tell from the skin –
the way it's clouding over, losing its ripe shine
in a mist of wrinkles. You can't actually see
the flesh go soft, the warm juice oozing free

of the cells. Yet if you really look
you know those cherries are already half-cooked –
just a shred of flesh clinging to dark stones,
a trickle of sweetness in a fold of the dunes.

Who can have dropped them – hopping, burning their soles
all the way to the water as the fruit still rolls
from the bag? Now almost naked, sitting side by side
and laughing, they spit pips into the creeping tide.

Imagine you come on them here, imagine your own mouth stained
with purple juice, and biting down on sand.

Rain

The hardest thing to do
must be rain slipping its silver skin
and bleeding to river as it slides downhill;
each wet stone is a well
you could fall into, each inverted tree
a circle of trapped sky.
The drops jump
on the surface like something alive.

And there's just one dry place
where stone is still itself
and reflects nothing, where a moment before
someone must have stood
breathing, with a glitter of fine rain
in the hair at her nape
before the first cold drop
shook itself and shivered and came down.

And now her skin's skin
is water. She's rushing downhill
to where the drowning trees
are black with birds. And what you've caught
is nothing
but paint on canvas
and a dry stone.

'Madam, I am the doctor, here is a banana.'

The canvas is almost empty
yet in this flat expanse
of blue the ghost of earth
turns in a spreading gleam:
a world,
a horizon,
sunrise holding its breath.

Years ago there was somewhere this blue –
where was it? – where little boys
wore sailor collars and sky
was luminous like this. If you close your eyes
you can hear gulls, a seaside town
with its people not yet gone;
a pedigree lapdog strains
and shivers at the leash. In a pinhole blur
the ferry's sleepy wash
still slaps at the jetty. On the quay
the roped-up luggage, netting, gutted fish.

It's what you'd call a blank screen
for anyone's animated cartoon
of the same title. A nifty doctor nips
from left to right,
his stethoscope streaming out
behind him like a tiny scarf.
And when he screeches to a stop
in a puff of epithets
we're meant to laugh.

Look closely. Can you see the fruit
half-peeled in his waistcoat pocket, sticking out?
And what do you make of that yellow,
does it mean something? And the blue
she's drowning in, the sky staining her pillow?

Yet when you take a step back
it's like peeling back skin
on something sweet and brown with bruises:
you can't not see it now – a woman's death
plays over and over
in ribbons of pith.

The title of the picture is a quotation from Nabokov's *Speak, Memory*

Circus Ring with Pig

And here are the clowns, of course,
in their exploding car
coughing its body-parts and honking
as they squirt a droopy downstroke
into dust. There are the trapezes
trembling overhead, the spangled dancer
mincing with tight buttocks
grey-grimed, end of a long season.
A chain of elephants
lumbers in small circles
trunk to tail, grey-fleshed and baggy
to a blast of rusty music
that's out of key, the trumpets
damp or damaged. Children
cobwebbed with candyfloss
yawn behind their hands.

And then the pig comes trotting
in through the canvas doorway,
rooting in the rank sawdust,
untroubled, pink as a dirty baby.
It lifts its hairless snout
and drools, sniffing and blinking
at the marks that swirl like writing
underfoot, the lights, the ladder
rising to the roof, the faces
waiting for something to happen.

Rugby

Somewhere out of sight they're warming up
under cloud to play in this grey-green field
framed by the skeletons of two enormous trees
stifled with ivy. Only the balls
pass over, egg-shaped, turning in the air
to land somewhere unseen in a gasp
of leather, mud and torn-up grass.
Just once or twice
a boy runs forward panting from one side
in black hooped yellow, angry as a wasp,
or gold as a buttercup
in mid-December. Then the trees suck him back
and the field's unpeopled. All you can see
are brown eggs falling round you out of the sky.

Moorland Figure in Poor Light

You can barely see him
against the brown of the hillside.
Mist fades out the crags, the fine detail
of path and lichened rock
you can only guess at. Low down,
there's a swell of bare trees, a rising puff
of birds, a winged shadow
that could lift and fly up, wheeling
somewhere beyond the frame.
And the single walker half-crouched
to the gradient, leaning, with all his weight
thrown forward, arm extended,
holding an invisible stick,
moves steadily uphill
where he'll lose his nose and mouth,
his shoulders, his clenched hand
on the knob, his knotted thighs,
till he's standing knee-deep
in a field of unbroken white
where tree-crowns shiny with damp,
outbuildings stacked for winter
with root crops, the river's silver thread
are a grey-white map
that fades even as he looks.
Somewhere inside the mist
a dog is barking, a woman's laugh
dies in a slam of doors, a sheep coughs.

Old Man with Chrysanthemums

Before the artist ruined him
with paint, I'd have taken his photograph –
a gaunt old man with a not-long-for-this-world face
full of flowers – two everlasting bunches
one pink, one yellow, every last petal smiling.

He shouldn't be standing here
with so few minutes, so many big flowers.
He should be hobbling home,
hoisting himself into a bus and easing himself down
to the kerb with his heavy bags and shuffling his way
up those last steep steps to where she is
quick in the kitchen and the steam rising
apron sticky with damp still grumbling

to give her flowers, bury her face in petals,
find scissors and slit the paper,
snap the rubber bands quick quick and snip
the stems so they can drink quickly
half a clear vase of water in less than two hours
and all the serrated leaves, the petals
stretching and unrolling in their smiling hundreds

cover his tired face as he rests them
here on the rail and waits at the street corner.

Blackberries

A mass of small black bubbles
in the foreground, their dark shine
reflecting light, a reddened leaf
you can almost see waving, and between
the hedge-plants you just glimpse
the glitter of sun on water –
boats at low tide, the clean lines of keels
beached and leaning, sand
carved into a little cliff
by receding ripples, blue nylon ropes, and stones.

It's not worth anything. Don't even bother to look.
A holiday photographer could do it
just as well – the quayside bench
banal as any bench, the water running out,
the fruit so like itself,
not worth the paint
– and yet

no human eye or camera could see
all this in focus in a single instant,
both the glistening fruit
you can almost crush against your tongue
in a spurt of juice, and the receding tide
in late afternoon, the leaning primrose boat
and that sky blue one
and the white,
the low sun slanting across slate,
couples clustered on benches talking.

A man calls to his dog
and the leaf waves, crimson, veined.

Portrait of a Leaf as Bird

How good of this small grey leaf
to pose as bird
so still in the middle of the road!

How kind not to fly away
as the artist approached,
to curb its sharp claws and beak

and let him paint leaf-as-bird
and bird-as-leaf
and put his irrelevant questions about flight

and stillness
seeing and not quite seeing
whether or not life is

feathered and wing-tip singing
and bird-brain lifted
small beating heart

or else this crumpled thing
he painted in careful shades
of grey, and brown.

Trees in High Wind

As if the undersides of leaves were fish, and the fish silver
like mist or moon and leaves were moving faster
than your eye could catch. As if something were floating,
rising to the surface, soon to be discovered –
the manes of horses streaming as they galloped
through weed that rippled rising in a green river.
As if the past were leaves and leaving and the still window
were still, and leaves were skin, and your skin younger.
As if your eyes half closed and the slit of light got brighter,
caught in liquid glass, flicking towards amber.
As if this blaze of white on grass were more than clover
and blue an unseen cloud, and cloud already half over –
the whole valley a green sea and the waves churning
and you a child in rough weather shouting louder and louder
as you sail into leaves, and come to no land ever.